# Barn Swallows

by J. Clark Sawyer

Consultant: Charles R. Brown
Department of Biological Sciences
University of Tulsa
Tulsa, Oklahoma

PUBLISHING

New York, New York

**Credits**

TOC, © Butterfly Hunter/Shutterstock; 4–5, © JJ Cadiz, Cajay/Wikipedia; 6–7, © Marie Read/
Photoshot; 7, © iStockphoto/Thinkstock; 8–9, © Patricia Fenn Gallery/Getty; 10, © iStockphoto/
Thinkstock; 12, © David Savory/Alamy; 13L, © Brian Bevan/ardea.com; 13R, © NHPA/Photoshot;
14–15, © CheepShot/Flickr Images; 16–17, © Biosphoto/Jean-Lou Zimmermann; 16, © Emil Von
Maltitz/Getty; 18–19, © Loic Poidevin/naturepl.com; 19, © Habicht, Michael/Animals Animals;
20–21, © Steve Gettle/Minden Pictures/Corbis; 22T, © iStockphoto/Thinkstock; 22M, © xpixel/
Shutterstock; 22B, © Chamelion Studio/Shutterstock; 23TL, © iStockphoto/Thinkstock; 23TR,
© Fuse/Thinkstock; 23BL, © Sophie Collin/Thinkstock; 23BR, © John Cancalosi/Alamy.

Publisher: Kenn Goin
Editor: Jessica Rudolph
Creative Director: Spencer Brinker
Design: Debrah Kaiser
Photo Researcher: Michael Win

*Library of Congress Cataloging-in-Publication Data*

Clark Sawyer, J., author.
  Barn swallows / by J. Clark Sawyer.
      pages cm. — (In winter, where do they go?)
  Includes bibliographical references and index.
  ISBN-13: 978-1-62724-314-8 (library binding)
  ISBN-10: 1-62724-314-3 (library binding)
  1. Barn swallow—Juvenile literature.  I. Title.
  QL696.P247C53 2015
  598.8'26—dc23
                                    2014009025

For more information, write to Bearport Publishing Company, Inc., 45 West 21st Street, Suite 3B,
New York, New York 10010. Printed in the United States of America.

10 9 8 7 6 5 4 3 2 1

# Contents

# Barn Swallows

It's a fall day in a park.

A barn swallow sits on a tree branch.

Soon it will start a long journey.

Some barn swallows build nests inside barns. This is how they got their name.

5

The little bird flies south for the winter. Why?

In winter, there is little food in northern parts of the world.

In the south, it is warmer.

There is more food.

Barn swallows eat **insects**, such as grasshoppers.

For months, the bird flies south.

It **migrates** with many other barn swallows.

Along the way, the birds rest.

Barn swallows may migrate in a group of more than one million birds!

By winter, the bird has reached its new home.

It has flown thousands of miles.

# Where Barn Swallows Live

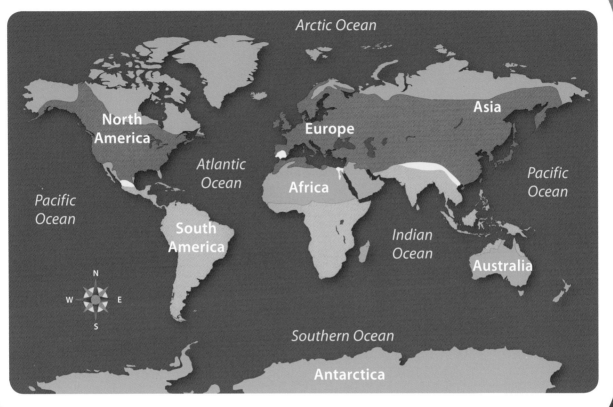

Arctic Ocean

North America

Europe

Asia

Atlantic Ocean

Pacific Ocean

Africa

Pacific Ocean

South America

Indian Ocean

Australia

N W E S

Southern Ocean

Antarctica

■ During Summer  ■ During Winter  ☐ All Year

Most barn swallows migrate. Only a few live in one area all year.

The bird finds lots of food in its winter home.

It zigzags in the air.

As it flies, it catches insects in its beak.

Barn swallows can drink as they fly above lakes and ponds. The birds scoop up water in their beaks.

14

During winter, the bird loses many of its feathers.

It grows new ones.

This is called **molting**.

Birds molt to replace damaged feathers. Molting helps prepare swallows for long trips.

In early spring, it gets warmer in the north.

The bird makes the long trip back.

Most barn swallows return to their northern homes by April.

nest

In the spring, barn swallows **mate**.

They gather mud and grass to build a nest.

Both the male and female swallows build the nest. The female bird lays three to seven eggs in it.

The babies hatch in June.

All summer, they grow stronger.

Soon, the young birds will take their first trip south.

Both parents bring food to their babies in the nest. When they are a few weeks old, the young swallows find food on their own.

# Barn Swallow Facts

There are more than 80 kinds of swallows. Barn swallows are the most common type. In winter, they live in fields and marshes. In summer, they may build their nests inside barns, under bridges, or on the outside of houses.

**Food:** Flies, grasshoppers, beetles, dragonflies, ants, butterflies, and moths

**Size:** 5.8 to 7.8 inches (14.7 to 20 cm) long, including tail feathers; wingspan is 11.4 to 13.5 inches (29 to 34.3 cm)

**Weight:** About 0.6 to 0.7 ounces (17 to 20 g)

**Life Span:** About four years

**Cool Fact:** Barn swallows have many different calls. Some calls warn other swallows that enemies, such as hawks or cats, are nearby.

Size of an adult barn swallow

A teacup

# Glossary

**insects** (IN-sekts) small animals that have six legs, three main body parts, two antennae, and a hard covering called an exoskeleton

**mate** (MAYT) to come together with another animal to have young

**migrates** (MYE-grayts) moves from one place to another at a certain time of the year

**molting** (MOHLT-ing) shedding outer skin, old feathers, or horns so that new ones can form

23

# Index

## Read More

**Crewe, Sabrina, and Malcolm Ellis.** *The Swallow.* Austin, TX: Raintree Steck-Vaughn (1997).

**Nelson, Robin.** *Migration (First Step Nonfiction: Discovering Nature's Cycles).* Minneapolis, MN: Lerner (2011).

## Learn More Online

To learn more about barn swallows, visit
**www.bearportpublishing.com/InWinterWhereDoTheyGo?**

## About the Author

J. Clark Sawyer lives in Connecticut. She has edited and written many books about history, science, and nature for children.